Alternator Books™

INDIGENOUS LANGUAGE REVITALIZATION

From Boarding Schools and Code Talkers to Immersion Learning

KATRINA M. PHILLIPS

Lerner Publications ◆ Minneapolis

For Leo and Max

Content consultant: Matthew J. Martinez

Copyright © 2025 by Lerner Publishing Group, Inc.

All rights reserved. International copyright secured. No part of this book may be reproduced, stored in a retrieval system, or transmitted in any form or by any means—electronic, mechanical, photocopying, recording, or otherwise—without the prior written permission of Lerner Publishing Group, Inc., except for the inclusion of brief quotations in an acknowledged review.

Lerner Publications Company
An imprint of Lerner Publishing Group, Inc.
241 First Avenue North
Minneapolis, MN 55401 USA

For reading levels and more information, look up this title at www.lernerbooks.com.

Main body text set in Aptifer Sans LT Pro Medium.
Typeface provided by Linotype AG.

Editor: Brianna Kaiser **Designer:** Athena Currier **Photo Editor:** Giliane Mansfeldt

Library of Congress Cataloging-in-Publication Data

Names: Phillips, Katrina M., author.
Title: Indigenous language revitalization : from boarding schools and code talkers to immersion learning / Katrina M. Phillips.
Description: Minneapolis : Lerner Publications , [2025]. | Series: Native rights (Alternator Books) | Includes bibliographical references and index. | Audience: Ages 8–12 | Audience: Grades 4–6 | Summary: "Many Indigenous languages were lost when the US and Canadian governments forced Indigenous children to learn and use English. Young readers will learn how Indigenous linguists and teachers are bringing these languages back to life"— Provided by publisher.
Identifiers: LCCN 2024012695 (print) | LCCN 2024012696 (ebook) | ISBN 9798765646915 (library binding) | ISBN 9798765661703 (paperback) | ISBN 9798765656716 (epub)
Subjects: LCSH: Indians of North America—Languages—Study and teaching—Juvenile literature. | Indians of North America—Languages—Revival—Juvenile literature.
Classification: LCC PM205 .P48 2025 (print) | LCC PM205 (ebook) | DDC 497.071—dc23/eng/20240627

LC record available at https://lccn.loc.gov/2024012695
LC ebook record available at https://lccn.loc.gov/2024012696

Manufactured in the United States of America
1-1010986-53132-7/15/2024

TABLE OF CONTENTS

INTRODUCTION Keeping Our Cultures Alive 4
CHAPTER 1 Boarding Schools 6
CHAPTER 2 Winning the War 12
CHAPTER 3 An Unbreakable Code 18
CHAPTER 4 Learning Our Languages 24

Glossary 30
Learn More 31
Index 32

INTRODUCTION
KEEPING OUR CULTURES ALIVE

Imagine you're at a summer camp. You learn songs, play games, and put on puppet shows. There's only one rule: you can't speak English.

For children of the Hoopa Valley Tribe in Northern California, language immersion camps help them learn the language of their ancestors. The camp brings their language, Na:tinixwe Mixine:whe, and their culture back to the people of the reservation.

For the Hupa, who call themselves Na:tinixwe, it's important that their children learn their language. The federal government built a school near the reservation in the late 1800s. Many elders of Indigenous nations, including the Na:tinixwe, were forced to attend federal Indian boarding schools as children. There, many of the children were punished if they spoke their Native languages.

When children left the schools, many of them could no longer speak their Native languages. And many were scared to teach their languages to their children. Over time, fewer people spoke these languages. In 2019 the Hoopa Valley Tribe estimated that only about twenty Na:tinixwe were fluent in their language.

Indigenous languages are about more than just words. They help explain cultural practices, keep ceremonies alive, and teach Indigenous peoples about their histories and their ways of life. Indigenous peoples across the country and around the world are working to save their languages. Immersion camps are just one way they're making it happen.

Some Indigenous peoples also use schools to teach their Native languages. Here, students at an Arapaho immersion school on the Wind River Reservation in Wyoming learn everything in the Arapaho language.

CHAPTER 1
Boarding Schools

Native parents, grandparents, and elders have educated their children for thousands of years. They have taught children how to care for and survive off their lands. Children have learned their histories, ceremonies, cultures, and languages.

But missionaries and US government officials didn't want Native peoples to live the way their ancestors had. The US government wanted to assimilate them. That meant the government wanted Native peoples to give up their ways of life, learn English, become Christian, and accept American values. Many Native peoples resisted.

Native children in the dining room at the Albuquerque Indian School, one of the off-reservation federal Indian boarding schools in the US, circa 1885

In the early 1800s, the government opened schools on reservations to assimilate Native children. But many of these children kept close ties with their families and communities.

Native children at the Carlisle Indian Industrial School, circa 1885

Separating Children from Families

In 1879 former military officer Richard Henry Pratt and the US government founded the Carlisle Indian Industrial School in Pennsylvania. It was the first off-reservation federal Indian boarding school. More off-reservation schools opened across the country.

Native children were forcibly removed from their homes and sent up to thousands of miles away from their families to live at these schools. Administrators cut off the students' long hair.

They gave the children American names, forced them to go to church and speak English, and punished them for speaking their Native languages. Hundreds of children died at these schools.

RESIDENTIAL SCHOOLS IN CANADA

In Canada, Christian churches and the Canadian government used residential schools to assimilate Indigenous children. There were more than 130 residential schools between 1831 and 1996. About 150,000 First Nation, Inuit, and Métis children were forced to attend these schools. The children were mistreated, and thousands of them died. Survivors of residential schools continue to call on the Canadian government to acknowledge the mistreatment students received at the schools.

The Kamloops Indian Residential School was one of the residential schools in Canada.

Lasting Impact

Many Native peoples refused to send their children away. In 1891 the government required children to attend these schools. Two years later, they allowed the Bureau of Indian Affairs to penalize parents who refused to send their children away. In 1894 the government sent nineteen Hopi men to the military prison on Alcatraz Island because they wouldn't send their children away.

Many Native children no longer spoke their Native languages after leaving the schools. Some of them only spoke

These Hopi men were sent to the military prison on Alcatraz Island for not sending their children to federal Indian boarding schools.

REFLECT

Think about the language or languages you use every day. Why are languages important? What are languages used for?

English out of fear since they'd been punished so harshly in school. Some of them no longer knew their languages and couldn't communicate with their relatives anymore.

In 2022 the US Department of the Interior released a report that said there were 408 federal Indian boarding schools between 1819 to 1969. This included twenty-one schools in Alaska and seven schools in Hawai'i.

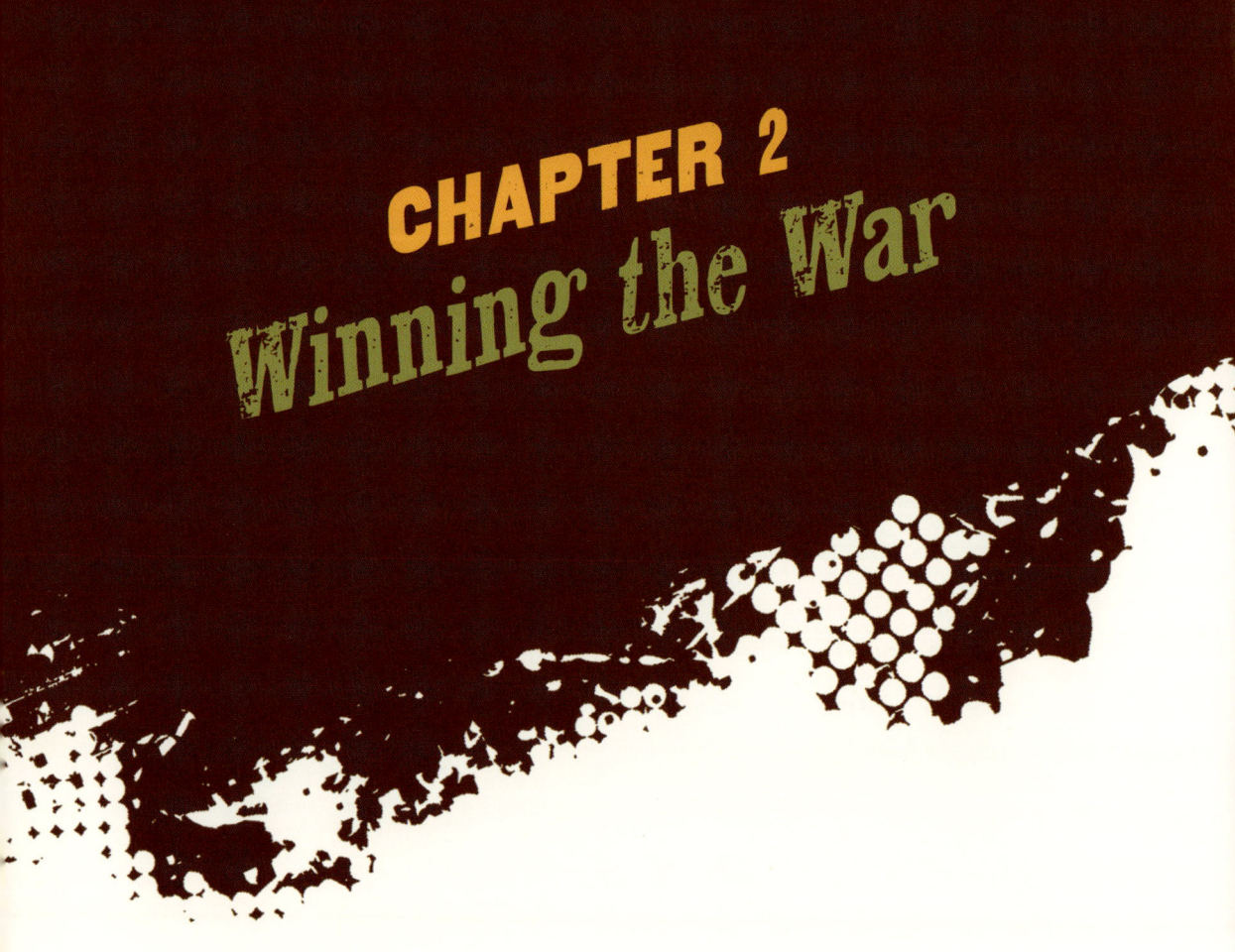

CHAPTER 2
Winning the War

During World War I (1914–1918), the United States joined forces with France, the United Kingdom, Russia, Italy, and Japan. They were the Allies and fought the Central powers. The Central powers were Germany, Austria-Hungary, the Ottoman Empire, and Bulgaria.

When the US entered the war in 1917, men across the country joined the military. About twelve thousand Native Americans joined.

An important part of the war took place on the western front. It ran from the border of Switzerland through France and Belgium to the North Sea. It was more than 400 miles (644 km) long.

The Allies struggled with communication on the western front in 1918. The runner system—where men would run from one point to another to share information—was slow and dangerous. Other systems such as radios and telephones didn't always work. The Germans were able to tap into the Allied telephone lines, take the Allied runners, and break every code the Allies created. This helped them uncover the Allied battle plans.

A map showing the main battle lines of the western front during World War I

REFLECT

When the 1924 Indian Citizenship Act passed, all Native Americans were granted US citizenship. Why do you think thousands of Native Americans served during World War I even if they weren't considered citizens?

A New Code

One day a captain heard two Allied soldiers talking. He couldn't understand a word the men were saying. He asked them what language they were speaking. The two soldiers were Choctaw, and they both spoke the Choctaw language.

The officer asked if any other Choctaw-speaking soldiers were around. The two men knew that some Choctaw soldiers were at the company headquarters, and they used a field telephone to send a message in Choctaw to them. The Choctaw soldiers at the headquarters quickly translated the message into English. Within hours, eight Choctaw-speaking soldiers had been sent out to help with communication. They also helped plan a series of attacks against the Germans.

Indigenous peoples also joined the Canadian military during World War I. Here, Mohawk soldiers serve on the western front.

The men became known as the Choctaw Telephone Squad. It grew to nineteen Choctaw soldiers. They created a code that the Germans couldn't understand. Since there weren't Choctaw translations for military words, they used other words. For example, they used the Choctaw term for "fast shooting gun" in place of "machine gun."

US soldiers operating a radio switchboard during World War I

This image includes some of the men that were part of the Choctaw Telephone Squad.

The Choctaw Telephone Squad is the most well-known use of a Native language in World War I. Cheyenne, Cherokee, Comanche, Ho-Chunk, Osage, and Yankton Sioux soldiers also used their Native languages in the war.

CHAPTER 3
An Unbreakable Code

The United States was part of the Allies again during World War II (1939–1945). The US, the United Kingdom, France, China, and the Soviet Union (a former nation made up of fifteen present-day countries) fought against the Axis powers. The Axis powers were Germany, Italy, and Japan.

Even more Native Americans joined the US military when the US entered World War II in 1941. The US Marine Corps recruited Navajo (also known as Diné) men who spoke both English and Navajo. They wanted the Navajo men to create an unbreakable code. Twenty-nine Navajo men became the first Navajo Code Talkers.

The original twenty-nine Navajo Code Talkers are sworn into the US Marine Corps in 1942.

The Navajo Code Talkers

The Navajo Code Talkers created Type One and Type Two Codes. For Type One Codes, they picked an English word that started with each letter of the alphabet. Then they translated that English word into Navajo. For the letter *C*, for example, they chose the English word *cat*, which is *moasi* in Navajo. Soldiers could then use *moasi* in a code in place of the letter *C*.

For Type Two Codes, the Code Talkers translated English words into Navajo. They created a dictionary of 411 words. For example, they translated the English military term *aircraft carrier* to the Navajo word *tsidi-moffa-ye-hi*, which means "bird carrier."

Navajo Code Talker Preston Toledo (*left*) and his cousin Frank Toledo use a field radio to send messages in Navajo.

Example of a Type One Navajo Code

Use the chart to translate the message. Can you crack the code? Check the answer at the bottom of the page to find out. (Hint: Turn each of the Navajo words into the letter of the English alphabet.)

English alphabet letter	Navajo word	English translation of Navajo word
C	MOASI	CAT
D	LHA-CHA-EH	DOG
E	DZEH	ELK
F	MA-E	FOX
I	TKIN	ICE
M	BE-TAS-TNI	MIRROR
N	A-CHIN	NOSE
O	NE-AHS-JAH	OWL
R	GAH	RABBIT

Message: **MOASI, NE-AHS-JAH, A-CHIN, MA-E, TKIN, GAH, BE-TAS-TNI, DZEH, LHA-CHA-EH**

Navajo Words and Military Terms

Military term	Navajo word	Literal English translation of Navajo word
BATTLESHIP	LO-TSO	WHALE
BOMBS	A-YE-SHI	EGGS
GRENADE	NI-MA-SI	POTATOES
SUBMARINE	BESH-LO	IRON FISH

*The information needed to create this code and translated military terms comes from the National Museum of the American Indian exhibit *Native Words, Native Warriors*.

Answer: Confirmed

After creating the code, they tested it. The officers gave the Code Talkers and the standard communications men a message to translate and send. It often took four hours to send messages the standard way. But the Code Talkers sent the message in less than three minutes. After months of practice, the Code Talkers were sent into battle.

The original Code Talkers served in important battles of the war. And enemies never broke their code. By the end of the war, hundreds of Navajo men had served as Code Talkers. Comanche, Hopi, and Meskwaki soldiers, among others, also served as Native American Code Talkers during the war.

REFLECT

Many of the Native American soldiers who served in World War I and World War II were forced to go to boarding schools as children. Why do you think the US government punished children for speaking their Native languages but wanted soldiers to speak their languages?

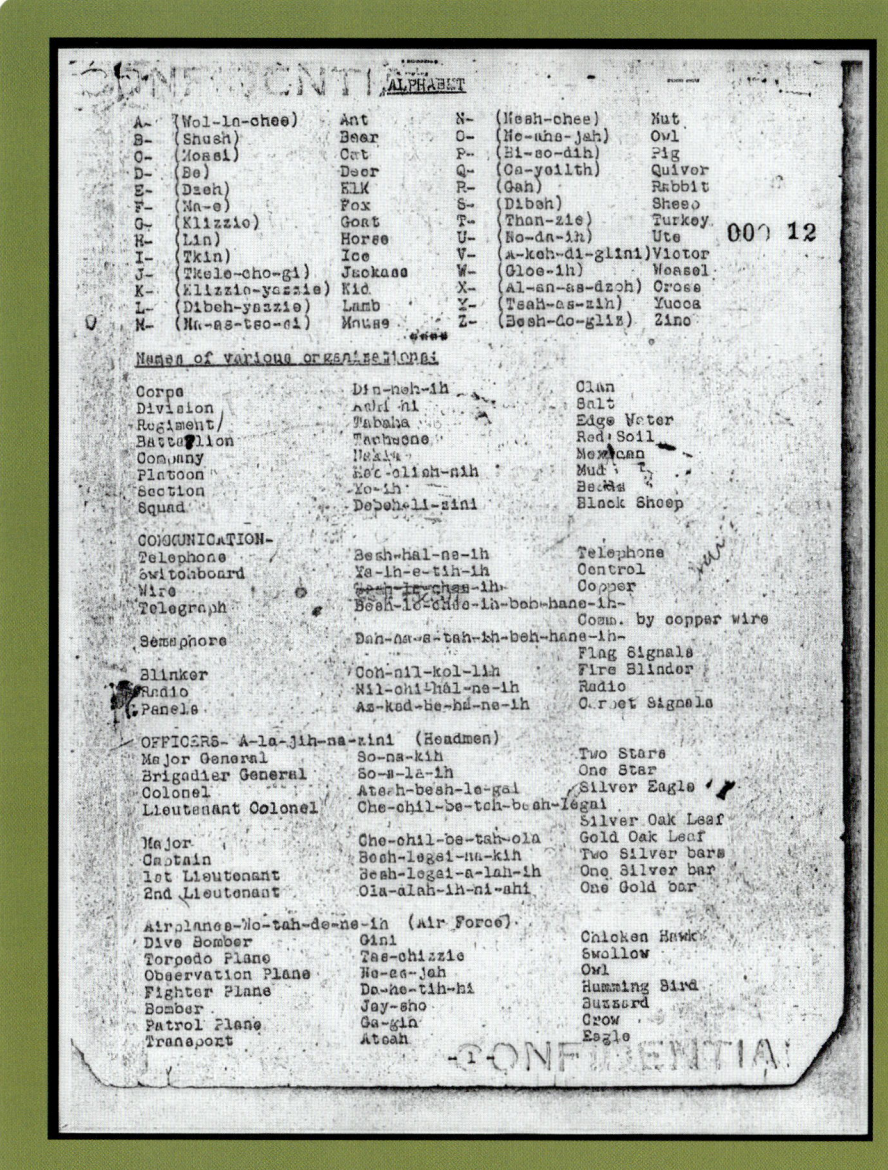

This is one of the declassified documents of the Navajo Code Talkers' code.

The Navajo Code Talkers were forbidden from telling anyone about their mission. The military kept the code classified until 1968.

CHAPTER 4
Learning Our Languages

As of January 2024, there are 574 federally recognized Indigenous nations in the US. But many Indigenous languages are endangered. These languages are at risk of being lost forever because fewer people know or will know how to speak them.

Language revitalization is important for many Indigenous nations. Summer camps and immersion schools are some of

A teacher instructs students at the New Kituwah Academy in 2014.

the ways these nations are working to save their endangered languages. And the US government has passed laws such as the Esther Martinez Native American Languages Preservation Act of 2006 to help support and fund Indigenous language programs.

Students learning at the New Kituwah Academy

Summer Camps and Immersion Schools

In northern Minnesota, the Red Lake Band of Chippewa hosts summer language camps. Students learn about plant medicines, lacrosse, and Ojibwe language and culture.

The New Kituwah Academy is a bilingual Cherokee and English school in Cherokee, North Carolina. Students at the school learn the Cherokee language, culture, traditions, and history. The Navajo Nation runs Tséhootsooí Diné Bi'Ólta' for children in kindergarten through sixth grade. Younger students are taught only in Navajo, while older students are taught in Navajo and English.

PLAINS INDIAN SIGN LANGUAGE (PISL)

Native peoples widely used PISL, or Hand Talk, for hundreds of years. Native nations that didn't have the same spoken languages were able to communicate by signing. But PISL was one of the languages Native children at boarding schools were punished for using. And many Deaf Native children were forced to use American Sign Language. Native peoples are working to save PISL, an endangered language.

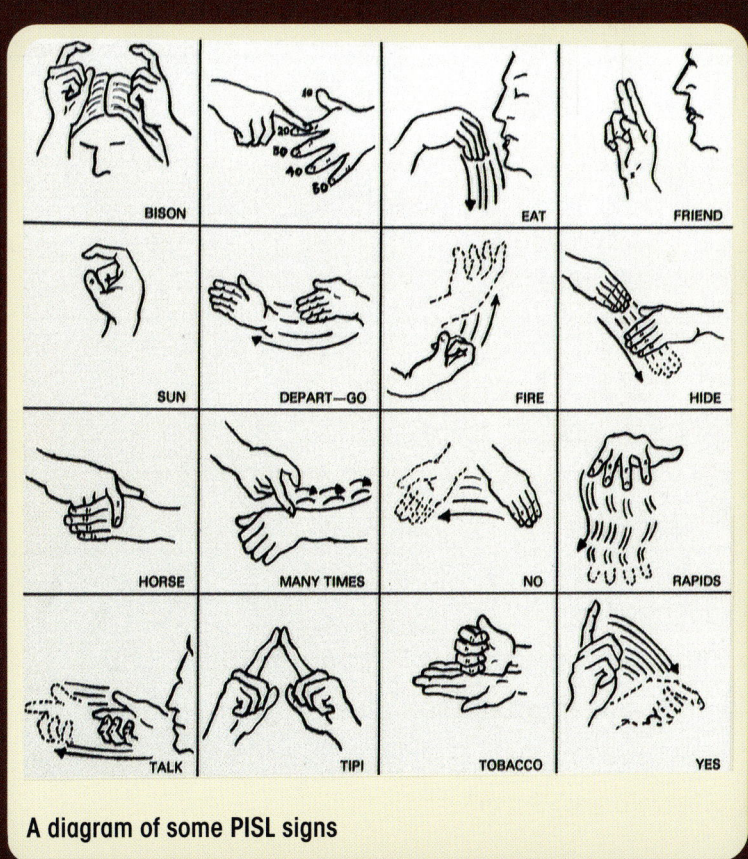

A diagram of some PISL signs

Waadookodaading is an Ojibwe immersion school in Wisconsin. Waadookodaading means "a place where people help each other" in the Ojibwe language. At the school, students learn the Ojibwe language, songs, ceremonies, and cultural practices such as making maple syrup. Local elders also share their knowledge with teachers and students at the school.

REFLECT

How are Indigenous language camps and immersion schools important and helpful to Indigenous communities?

Amoni Moss, Brock Bearing, and Santianna Gracielle Mendoza attend an Arapho immersion school in 2017.

In Minneapolis, Minnesota, students at Bdote Learning Center can enroll in either Ojibwe or Dakota immersion. On the Leech Lake Indian Reservation in north-central Minnesota, students at the Bug-O-Nay-Ge-Shig School learn to do everything in Ojibwe—including math.

Indigenous peoples are fighting to keep their languages alive. It's not always easy. The painful history of boarding schools makes it challenging. But from boarding schools to Native codes to immersion schools, Indigenous languages and Indigenous peoples have survived.

Glossary

ancestor: a person from whom someone is descended

assimilate: becoming similar to others by taking in and using their customs and culture

classified: kept private or withheld from the general public

culture: the beliefs, customs, and languages of a group of people

endangered: a language that is at risk of no longer being used

fluent: able to easily speak a language

immersion: a method of learning a second language

language revitalization: to prevent or reverse the decline of a language

missionary: a person sent by a church or religious group to teach or convert other people to their religion

reservation: an area of land reserved for a tribe or tribes under treaty or other agreement with the United States or Canada. There are more than three hundred reservations in the United States.

translate: to convert words into another language

Learn More

Bellanger DeGroat, Cayla. *Indigenous Cultures Today: Protecting Native Families and Practicing Cultural Traditions*. Minneapolis: Lerner Publications, 2025.

Britannica Kids: Native Boarding Schools
https://kids.britannica.com/students/article/Native-boarding-schools/636007

Buckley, James, Jr. *Who Were the Navajo Code Talkers?* New York: Penguin Workshop, 2021.

Choctaw Nation of Oklahoma: Code Talkers
https://www.choctawnation.com/about/history/code-talkers/

Francis, III, Lee, Arigon Starr, Janet Miner, Lee Francis IV, Roy Boney Jr., Jonathan Nelson, Renee Nejo, and Weshoyot Alvitr. *Tales of the Mighty Code Talkers*. New York: Reycraft Books, 2020.

National Museum of the American Indian: Code Talkers
https://americanindian.si.edu/static/why-we-serve/topics/code-talkers/

National Museum of the American Indian: Struggling with Cultural Repression
https://americanindian.si.edu/nk360/code-talkers/boarding-schools/

Time for Kids: Honoring Navajo Code Talkers
https://www.timeforkids.com/g56/honoring-navajo-code-talkers/

Index

Alcatraz Island, 10
Allies, 12–14, 18
assimilation, 6–7, 9

Carlisle Indian Industrial School, 8
Choctaw Telephone Squad, 14–17

endangered languages, 24–25, 27

federal Indian boarding schools, 4–5, 8–11, 22, 27

Hoopa Valley Tribe, 4–5

immersion camps, 4–5, 24, 26, 28
immersion schools, 24, 26, 28–29

Navajo Code Talkers, 18–23

Plains Indian Sign Language (PISL), 27

residential schools, 9

translations, 15–16, 19–20, 22

western front, 12–13

Photo Acknowledgments

Image credits: Joe Amon/The Denver Post/Getty Images, p. 5; Graphic House/Archive Photos/Getty Images, p. 7; Wikimedia Commons PD, p. 8; Chris Allan/Alamy, p. 9; TradingCardsNPS/flickr (CC BY 2.0), p. 10; Antiqua Print Gallery/Alamy, p. 13; Everett Collection Historical/Alamy, p. 15; AP Photo, p. 16; Wikimedia Commons PD, p. 17; Alpha Historica/Alamy; pp. 18, 19; Northern Arizona University. Cline Library, p. 23; Neddy1234 / Wikimedia Commons (CC BY-SA 3.0), pp. 25, 26; public domain sourced/access rights from kimber/Alamy, p. 27; Joe Amon/The Denver Post /Getty Images, p. 29; Design elements: kiwihug/Unsplash; Miloje/Shutterstock; Archiwiz/Shutterstock; mikesj11/Shutterstock.

Cover: aljosa2015/Shutterstock; grynold/Shutterstock.